*Edited and Translated*
*by Lucien Stryk and Takashi Ikemoto*
*with an*
*introduction by Lucien Stryk*

# The Penguin Book of Zen Poetry

*The Swallow Press Inc.*
*Chicago*

THE SWALLOW PRESS
811 West Junior Terrace
Chicago, Illinois 60613

First published 1977

Foreword and Introduction copyright © Lucien Stryk, 1977
A Note on the Translation copyright © Takashi Ikemoto, 1977
The poems in Part Two,
'Poems of the Japanese Zen Masters', are from
*Zen: Poems, Prayers, Sermons, Anecdotes, Interviews,*
translations copyright © Lucien Stryk and Takashi Ikemoto,
1963, 1965, published by Doubleday & Co.
All remaining translations
copyright © Lucien Stryk and Takashi Ikemoto, 1977

ISBN 0–8040–0792–6

Library of Congress Catalog Card Number 77–832–37

Set in Monotype Fournier
Printed in Great Britain by Cox & Wyman Ltd, Fakenham
Designed by Gerald Cinamon

*To the memory of my cousin Stephen Ullmann*
  – Lucien Stryk

*To the memory of my beloved brother Yukio*
  – Takashi Ikemoto

The temple, reached by a narrow mountain path five miles from the bus stop, was in one of the most beautiful districts of Japan. Surrounded by blazing maples, it appeared to have been rooted there for centuries. To its right was a kiln with a batch of fresh-fired pots, to its left a large vegetable garden where a priest bent giving full attention to a radish patch. He greeted me warmly and at once asked me to stay the night. Talk would wait till evening, after his meeting with parishioners – farmers, woodsmen – to discuss a coming festival. Each, I noticed, brought an offering – fruit, eggs, chestnuts. That time I came with nothing. Twenty years later I brought a book of Zen poems, one of a number translated since that first inspiring meeting.

Poetry had always been part of my life, and my interest in Zen poetry began as the result of that visit. Moved by a show of ceramics, calligraphy and haiku poems in Niigata, while teaching there, I asked a friend to take me to the artist. The evening of my visit I discovered that the priest's life was devoted equally to parish, ceramics and poetry. He spoke with love of haiku poets, Basho, Issa, and mentioned great Zen masters who excelled in poetry – Dogen, Bunan, Hakuin, names unfamiliar to me.

I was intrigued when he compared their work to certain Western poets (he especially admired the passage from Whitman in the Introduction), and I resolved to learn something of Zen poetry. He was wonderfully impressive then, and I found him even more so now, this priest-artist content with earth, pots and poems, seeking no praise of the world, his deepest care the people around him. I have owed him all these years a debt of gratitude, both for my feelings about Zen and for the lesson that one should make the most of the earth under one's feet, whether Japan or midland America, which have stemmed in large measure from our meeting.

My second lectureship in Japan, some years after, was in Yamaguchi, the 'Kyoto of the West'. There, at the Joei Temple, where the great painter Sesshu had served as priest in the fifteenth century, came another meeting which would leave its mark. Takashi Ikemoto, a colleague at the university, and I were interviewing the master of the temple for what later became our first volume of translation from Zen literature. I said things about the rock garden behind the temple, laid down by Sesshu – surely one of the finest in Japan – which struck the master as shallow. He patiently explained that in order to grasp the meaning of so great a work of Zen, I would have to meditate, experience the garden with my being. I was intrigued and humbled: familiar, through translating the literature, with the ways of Zen masters, I accepted his reproval as challenge. Thus I began a sequence of poems on Sesshu's garden, a discovering of things which made possible not only a leap into a truer poetry of my own but also more effective rendering of Zen poems.

Years and Zen books since, I still think of those encounters as phases of rebirth. Now, after meetings with Zen masters, poets and artists, comes this volume, the poems translated in homage to those Zennists who insist that awakened life is not a birthright but something to be won through, along a way beyond the self. My experiences, however ordinary and lacking drama they may be, I give here because they are the kind which have always been important to Zen – leading to awareness of possibilities for art and life which, as the poems reveal, are limitless.

LUCIEN STRYK

## I

The Golden Age of China, T'ang through Sung dynasties (AD 618–1279), began not long after the Western Roman Empire came to an end and lasted well beyond the First Crusade. One of the most cultivated eras in the history of man, its religious, philosophical and social ground had been prepared centuries before Christianity, and men perfected their lives and arts certain that they gave meaning to something higher than themselves. To artists of the time, numerous and skilled, poetry and painting were Ways – two among many, to be sure, but glorious Ways – to realization of Truth, whose unfolding made possible not only fulfilled life but calm acceptance of its limitations. They saw in the world a process of becoming, yet each of its particulars, at any moment of existence, partook of the absolute. This meant that no distinction was drawn between the details of a landscape – cliffs, slopes, estuaries, waterfalls – shaped by the artist's emotions. Foreground, background, each was part of the process, in poetry as in painting, the spirit discovering itself among the things of this world.

> *On the rocky slope, blossoming*
> *Plums – from where?*
> *Once he saw them, Reiun*
> *Danced all the way to Sandai.*
>
> HOIN

The artist's visions were held to be revelatory; painting, poem meant to put men in touch with the absolute. Judgement of art works was made principally with that in mind.

Some might delight the senses, a few exalt the spirit, whose role was taken for granted to be paramount, the greatest artists respecting its capacity to discover itself anew in their works. Over centuries the West has deduced the guiding aesthetic principle of such art to be 'Less is More', and a number of stories bear this out.

One concerns a painting competition in the late T'ang dynasty, a time of many such events and gifted competitors, all of whom, brought up in an intellectual and artistic meritocracy, were aware of what success might mean. Judged by master painters, most carefully arranged, each had its theme, that of our story being 'Famous Monastery in the Mountains'. Ample time was provided for the participants to meditate before taking up brushes. More than a thousand entries of monasteries in sunlight, in shadow, under trees, at mountain-foot, on slopes, at the very peak, by water, among rocks – all seasons. Mountains of many sizes, shapes, richly various as the topography itself. Since the monastery was noted 'famous', monks abounded, working, praying, all ages and conditions. The competition produced works destined to be admired for centuries to come. The winning painting had no monastery at all: a monk paused, reflecting, on a misty mountain bridge. Nothing – everything – more. Evoking atmosphere, the monk knew his monastery hovered in the mist, more beautiful than hand could realize. To define, the artist must have learnt from the Taoism of Lao Tzu or the Zen of Hui-neng, is to limit.

## II

Zen began its rapid growth in early T'ang China, a product of the merging of the recently introduced Buddhism of the Indian monk Bodhidharma, who reached China in 520, and

Taoism, the reigning philosophy of poets and painters for some thousand years. Providing a rigorously inspiring discipline, insisting on the primacy of meditation, its temples and monasteries were havens for seekers after truth throughout the T'ang, Sung and Mongol-shadowed Yuan dynasties. Zen masters, religious guides, often themselves poets and painters, made judgements concerning the spiritual attainments of artist-disciples on the basis of works produced. Neither before nor since has art had so important a role in community life, and there are countless instances of poems or paintings affecting the development of the philosophy itself. One such concerns the Sixth Patriarch Hui-neng, who was named as Hung-jen's successor chiefly on the strength of his famous enlightenment poem:

> *The tree of Perfect Wisdom*
> *Was originally no tree,*
> *Nor has the bright mirror*
> *Any frame. Buddha-nature*
> *Forever clear and pure,*
> *Where is there any dust?*

Writers of such poems did not think themselves poets. Rather they were gifted men – masters, monks, some lay-men – who after momentous experiences found themselves with something to say which only a poem could express. Enlightenment, point of their meditation, brought about transformation of the spirit; a poem was expected to convey the essential experience and its effect. Such an awakening might take years of unremitting effort, to most it would never come at all:

One day Baso, disciple of Ejo, the Chinese master, was asked by the master why he spent so much time meditating.

Baso: 'To become a Buddha.'

The master lifted a brick and began rubbing it very hard. It was now Baso's turn to ask a question: 'Why,' he asked, 'do you rub that brick?'

'To make a mirror.'

'But surely,' protested Baso, 'no amount of polishing will change a brick into a mirror.'

'Just so,' the master said: 'no amount of cross-legged sitting will make *you* into a Buddha.'

Yet masters did their best to guide disciples: one device was the *koan* (problem for meditation), which they were asked to solve. As no logical solution was possible, the meditator was always at wits' end – the intention. One of the *koans*, usually first given, was Joshu's 'Oak in the courtyard', based on the master's answer to the standard Zen question 'What's the meaning of Bodhidharma's coming to China?' These awakening poems, responses to this question of the masters, suggest the range of possibilities:

> *Joshu's 'Oak in the courtyard' –*
> *Nobody's grasped its roots.*
> *Turned from sweet plum trees,*
> *They pick sour pears on the hill.*

EIAN

> *Joshu's 'Oak in the courtyard'*
> *Handed down, yet lost in leafy branch*
> *They miss the root. Disciple Kaku shouts –*
> *'Joshu never said a thing!'*

MONJU-SHINDO

Given their importance, it is not surprising to find in early Chinese enlightenment poems frequent references to *koans*. Most poems, though, deal with major aims of the philosophy, escape from space-time bondage, for example, a hard-won precondition of awakening:

> *Twenty years a pilgrim,*
> *Footing east, west.*
> *Back in Seiken,*
> *I've not moved an inch.*
>
> SEIKEN-CHIJU

> *Earth, river, mountain:*
> *Snowflakes melt in air.*
> *How could I have doubted?*
> *Where's north? south? east? west?*
>
> DANGAI

Many express swift release from conventional attachments:

> *Searching Him took*
> *My strength.*
> *One night I bent*
> *My pointing finger –*
> *Never such a moon!*
>
> KEPPO

Need for such release, transcending of doctrine (finger pointing at the moon, never taken for the moon itself), was the theme of Bodhidharma's historical interview with Emperor Wu of Liang, shortly after his arrival in China (by then some schools of Buddhism had been established there a few hundred years):

Emperor Wu: From the beginning of my reign, I have built many temples, had numerous sacred books copied, and supported all the monks and nuns. What merit have I?
Bodhidharma: None.

Emperor Wu: Why?

Bodhidharma: All these are inferior deeds, showing traces of worldliness, but shadows. A truly meritorious deed is full of wisdom, but mysterious, its real nature beyond grasp of human intelligence – something not found in worldly achievement.

Emperor Wu: What is the first principle of your doctrine?

Bodhidharma: Vast emptiness, nothing holy.

Emperor Wu: Who, then, stands before me?

Bodhidharma: I don't know.

Not long after this Bodhidharma wrote his famous poem:

> *Transmission outside doctrine,*
> *No dependencies on words.*
> *Pointing directly at the mind,*
> *Thus seeing oneself truly,*
> *Attaining Buddhahood.*

As might be expected, awakening poems were held precious in Zen communities, serving for generations as *koans* themselves or as subjects for *teisho* (sermons). Interpretation was often made in the light of the master's life, what led to his experience. Nan-o-Myo, awakened when asked by his master to interpret 'Not falling into the law of causation, yet not ignoring it', wrote:

> *Not falling, not ignoring –*
> *A pair of mandarin ducks*
> *Alighting, bobbing, anywhere.*

Every utterance of a worthy master was thought significant. The late Sung master Tendo-Nyojo, an example, guided Japan's great Dogen (1200–1253) to enlightenment, which alone made his death poem, simple as it is, glorious to the Japanese:

> *Sixty-six years*
> *Piling sins,*
> *I leap into hell –*
> *Above life and death.*

Zen death poems, remarkable in world literature, have a very ancient tradition. On their origin one can only speculate, but probably in early communities masters felt responsibility to disciples beyond the grave, and made such poems in the hope that they would help point the way to attainment, not only for disciples but for posterity. To some the final poem was not felt to be itself of much importance:

> *Life's as we*
> *Find it – death too.*
> *A parting poem?*
> *Why insist?*
>
> DAIE-SOKO

Many, however, considered it to be a symbolic summation, quite possibly preparing well before the inevitable moment. It would stand, every syllable pondered, and lives might well be affected by truth, absolute, whatever its message and worth as 'poetry'. Differences between death poems give a sense of the variety of temperament among Chinese masters. Fuyo-Dokai's vital self-assurance:

> *Seventy-six: done*
> *With this life –*
> *I've not sought heaven,*
> *Don't fear hell.*
> *I'll lay these bones*
> *Beyond the Triple World,*
> *Unenthralled, unperturbed.*

Koko's sense of release from a harsh existence:

> *The word at last,*
> *No more dependencies:*
> *Cold moon in pond,*
> *Smoke over the ferry.*

Shozan's astringent mockery:

> *'No mind, no Buddha,'*
> *Disciples prattle.*
> *'Got skin, got marrow.'*
> *Well, goodbye to that.*
> *Beyond, peak glows on peak!*

There is no way of telling, records being scant and unreliable (there are wild variants of birth and death dates), whether all wrote death poems, but given their solemn purpose they probably did. By 1279, when China was overrun by Mongols, Zen had flourished for almost one hundred years in Japan. There from the start death poems of masters were thought to have great religious meaning. Dogen left, exulting:

> *Four and fifty years*
> *I've hung the sky with stars.*
> *Now I leap through –*
> *What shattering!*

## III

Centuries before the introduction of Zen in the Kamakura Period (1192–1333), Japan had been virtually transformed by Chinese Buddhism. Every aspect of life, from the Nara Period (710–84) on, reflected in one way or another the Chinese world vision. Painters and poets looked to China constantly, as did the greatest painter in the Chinese style, Sesshu, who crossed there for instruction and inspiration. Not all became Zennists like Sesshu, who was to join the priesthood, but most were guided by the philosophy, their works revealing the extent. In the earliest Zen communities enlightenment and death poems were written strictly in *kanji* (Chinese characters), in classical verse forms preferred by the Chinese masters – there is little to distinguish poems of the first Japanese Zennists from those written in China centuries before.

Here is the master Daito's enlightenment poem, written when he had succeeded in solving the eighth *koan* of the Chinese classic Zen text *Hekiganroku*, which contains a reference to 'Unmon's barrier':

> *At last I've broken Unmon's barrier!*
> *There's exit everywhere – east, west; north, south.*
> *In at morning, out at evening; neither host nor guest.*
> *My every step stirs up a little breeze.*

And here is Fumon's death poem:

> *Magnificent! Magnificent!*
> *No one knows the final word.*
> *The ocean bed's aflame,*
> *Out of the void leap wooden lambs.*

The Japanese masters composed not only enlightenment and death poems in Chinese verse forms, they often wrote of important events in the history of Zen, like Bodhidharma's interview with the Emperor Wu. Here is Shunoku's poem on the subject. ('Shorin' is the temple where Bodhidharma, on discovering that the emperor lacked insight, sat in Zen for nine years. To reach the temple he had to cross the Yangtze River.)

*After the spring song, 'Vast emptiness, no holiness',*
*Comes the song of snow-wind along the Yangtze River.*
*Late at night I too play the noteless flute of Shorin,*
*Piercing the mountains with its sound, the river.*

Even in writing on general themes associated with Zen life the masters employed the purest literary Chinese. Since only few Japanese knew the language, this practice made the Zen poems élitist, leading to the feeling on the part of masters like Dogen that an indigenous verse form, *tanka* (or *waka*), should be utilized. Such works would be understood in and out of the Zen communities, and surely it was possible to be as inspiring in Japanese, which, though using *kanji*, had a syllabary and was very different from Chinese. The most important collection of early Japanese poetry, the *Manyoshu* (eighth century), contains three kinds of verse forms: *choka, tanka* and *sedoka*, all based on arrangements of 5-7-5 syllable lines, the most popular, *tanka*, structured as 5-7-5-7-7 syllables – strictly, without any possible variation.

In the Heian Period (794–1185), which immediately preceded the first age of Zen, *tanka* was the favourite verse form at the courts. Towards the end of Heian, *renga* (linked verse), became popular: a chain of alternating 14 and 21 syllables independently composed but associated with the verses coming before and after. By the fifteenth century, *renga* expiring of artificiality, something more vital was found, the *haikai renga*, linked verses of 17 syllables. Later came individual poems of 17 syllables, *haiku*, the earliest authentic examples by writers like Sogi (1421–1502), Sokan (1458–1546) and Moritake (1472–1549).

Basho, thought by many Japanese to be their finest *haiku* writer and greatest poet, lived from 1644 to 1694. Like almost all noted *haiku* writers he was a Zennist, practising discipline under the master Butcho, with whom, according to Dr D. T. Suzuki, he had the following exchange:

Butcho: How are you getting along these days?
Basho: Since the recent rain moss is greener than ever.
Butcho: What Buddhism was there before the moss became green?

Resulting in enlightenment and the first of his best-known *haiku*:

Basho: Leap-splash – a frog.

Whether or not they undertook discipline, *haiku* writers thought themselves living in the spirit of Zen, their truest poems expressing its ideals. To art lovers the appeal of *haiku* is not unlike that of a *sumie* (ink-wash) scroll by Sesshu, and many *haiku* poets, like Buson, were also outstanding painters.

Zennists have always associated the two arts: 'When a feeling reaches its highest pitch,' says Dr Suzuki, Zen's most distinguished historian, 'we remain silent, even 17 syllables may be too many. Japanese artists . . . influenced by the way of Zen tend to use the fewest words or strokes of brush to express their feelings. When they are too fully expressed no room for suggestion is possible, and suggestibility is the secret of the Japanese arts.' Like a painting or rock garden, *haiku* is an object of meditation, drawing back the curtain on essential truth. It shares with other arts qualities belonging to the Zen aesthetic – simplicity, naturalness, directness, profundity – and each poem has its dominant mood: *sabi* (isolation), *wabi* (poverty), *aware* (impermanence) or *yugen* (mystery).

If it is true that the art of poetry consists in saying important things with the fewest possible words, then *haiku* has a just place in world literature. The limitation of syllables assures terseness and concision, and the range of association in the finest examples is at times astonishing. It has the added advantage of being accessible: a seasonal reference, direct or indirect, simplest words, chiefly names of things in dynamic relationships, familiar themes, make it under-standable to most, on one level at least. The *haiku* lives most fully in nature, of great meaning to a people who never feel it to be outside themselves. Man is fulfilled only when unseparated from his surroundings, however hostile they may appear:

> *To the willow —*
> *all hatred, and desire*
> *of your heart.*
>
> BASHO

> *White lotus —*
> *the monk*
> *draws back his blade.*
>
> BUSON

> *Under cherry trees*
> *there are*
> *no strangers.*
>
> ISSA

In the West, perhaps as a result of fascination with the *haiku* (its association with the development of modern poetry at one extreme, its universal appeal in schools at the other), it arouses as much suspicion as admiration. It looks so easy, something anyone can do. A most unfortunate view, for *haiku* is a quintessential form, much like the sonnet in Elizabethan England, being precisely suited to (as it is the product of) Japanese sensibility, conditioned by

Zen. For Basho, Buson, Issa, *haiku* permitted the widest possible field of discovery and experimentation.

The Zen experience is centripetal, the artist's contemplation of subject sometimes referred to as 'mind-pointing'. The disciple in an early stage of discipline is asked to point the mind at (meditate upon) an object, say a bowl of water. At first he is quite naturally inclined to metaphorize, expand, rise imaginatively from water to lake, sea, clouds, rain. Natural perhaps, but just the kind of 'mentalization' Zen masters caution against. The disciple is instructed to continue until it is possible to remain strictly with the object, penetrating more deeply, no longer looking *at* it but, as the Sixth Patriarch Hui-neng maintained essential, *as* it. Only then will he attain the state of *muga*, so close an identification with object that the unstable mentalizing self disappears. The profoundest *haiku* give a very strong sense of the process:

> *Dew of the bramble,*
> *thorns*
> *sharp white.*
>
> BUSON

> *Arid fields,*
> *the only life —*
> *necks of cranes.*
>
> SHIKO

To give an idea of the way *haiku* work, without making an odious cultural comparison, here is Ezra Pound's 'In a Station of the Metro', perhaps the most admired (and for good reason) *haiku*-like poem in English:

> *The apparition of these faces in the crowd;*
> *Petals on a wet, black bough.*

A simile, the poem startles as *haiku* often do, but much of what is said would, to a *haiku* poet, be implied. Incorporating the title (*haiku* are never titled), he might make the poem read:

> *Faces in the metro –*
> *petals*
> *on a wet black bough.*

If asked why, he might answer: the first few words, 'The apparition of these', though sonorous enough, add nothing. Nor does the reference to 'crowd', metro 'stations' usually being crowded – besides, the 'petals' of the simile would make that clear. His revision, he might claim, transforms the piece into an acceptable *haiku*, one rather like, perhaps less effective than, Onitsura's:

> *Autumn wind –*
> *across the fields,*
> *faces.*

Without using simile, Onitsura stuns with an immediacy of vision – those faces whipped by a cold wind.

For centuries *haiku* has been extremely popular, and there are established schools with widely differing views. Typical is the Tenro, truly traditional, working with the 5-7-5 syllabic pattern, clear seasonal reference, and possessing a creed – *Shasei*, on-the-spot composition with the subject 'traced to its origin'. There are around two thousand members all over Japan, and it is usual for groups to meet at a designated spot, often a Zen temple, and write as many as one hundred *haiku* in a night, perhaps only one of which, after months of selection and revision, will be adequate. It will then be sent to one of the school's masters and considered for the annual anthology, representing poems of some thirty members.

Untypical by comparison is the Soun (free-verse) school, which feels no obligation to stick to the 17-syllable pattern. Short and compact, however, its poems are written in the 'spirit of Basho'. Their creed is more general – Significance – and is very close to Zen, many of the members involved in discipline. They follow an ancient dictum, *Zenshi ichimi* (Poetry and Zen are one), and *Kado*, the Way of Poetry. As they strive for the revelatory, fewer poems are written than in the Tenro. Both schools, while opposed in principle, relate *haiku* to Zen, as do all other schools. Yet very few contemporary *haiku* could have pleased Basho, for however lofty the ideals they are generally derivative.

*Kado*, the Way of poetry to self-discovery, is similar in aim to other *do* (Ways) of Zen: *Gado* (painting), *Shodo* (calligraphy), *Jindo* (philosophy), *Judo* (force). *Haiku* teachers and Zen masters expect no miracles of disciples, yet maintain that with serious practice of an art, given aspirations, men perfect themselves: farmers, professors make their *haiku*, most egalitarian of arts. To those who find art a mystery engaged in by the chosen, the sight of a *haiku*-school group circling an autumn bush, lined notebooks, pens in hand, can be sharply touching. Only a cynic would think otherwise.

The few of course achieve true distinction in the skill, and are known to all who care for poetry. Usually they echo early masters, but some find that language cramping and consciously introduce the modern – factories, tractors, automobiles. They will admit, without derogating, to taking little pleasure from old *haiku*. They are however generous readers of each other's work and that of certain contemporary poets. One in whom many are interested, despite his not being a writer of *haiku*, is Shinkichi Taka-hashi, regarded throughout Japan as the greatest living Zen poet.

## IV

Overlooking the sea in a fishing village on Shikoku Island, a poem is carved on a stone:

> ABSENCE
> *Just say, 'He's out' –*
> *back in*
> *five billion years!*

It is Shinkichi Takahashi's voice we hear. He was born in 1901, and the commemorative stone, placed by his towns-men, is one of many honours accorded him in recent years: another is the Ministry of Education's prestigious Prize for Art, awarded for *Collected Poems* (1973). In Japan poets are often honoured in this way, but rarely one as anarchical as Takahashi. He began as a Dadaist, publishing the novel *Dada* in 1924, and defied convention thereafter. Locked up in his early life a few times for 'impulsive actions', when his newly printed *Dadaist Shinkichi's Poetry* was handed to him through the bars of a police cell, he tore it into shreds.

In 1928 Takahashi began serious Zen study under the master Shizan Ashikaga at the Shogenji Rinzai Temple, known for severity of discipline. He trained for seventeen long years, doing *zazen* (formal sitting in meditation) and studying *koans* – on which he wrote numerous poems. He attained enlightenment (*satori*) the first time on reaching the age of forty. In 1953, when fifty-two, he was given *inka* (his awakening testified to) by Shizan, one of six or seven disciples so honoured. In addition to some fiction and much poetry, he has written books on Zen highly regarded by Zennists, among them *Stray Notes on Zen Study* (1958), *Mumonkan* (1958), *Rinzairoku* (1959) and *A Life of Master Dogen* (1963).

Takahashi has interested fellow-poets and critics, East and West. A Japanese poet writes:

Takahashi's poetry is piquancy itself, just as Zen, the quintessence of Buddhism, bawls out by means of its concise vocabulary a sort of piquant ontology . . . Where does this enlivened feature come from? It comes from his strange disposition which enables him to sense the homogeneity of all things, including human beings. It is further due to his own method of versification: he clashes his idea of timelessness against the temporality of all phenomena to cause a fissure, through which he lets us see personally and convincingly the reality of limitless space.

The American poet Jim Harrison comments in the *American Poetry Review* on his 'omniscience about the realities that seems to typify genius of the first order', and goes on:

Nothing is denied entrance into these poems . . . All things are in their minutely suggestive proportions, and given an energy we aren't familiar with . . . Part of the power must come from the fact that the poet has ten thousand centers as a Zennist, thus is virtually centerless.

Philosophical insight is uncommon enough, but its authentic expression in poetry is extremely rare, whether found in T. S. Eliot's 'Four Quartets' or in Shinkichi Takahashi's 'Shell':

*Nothing, nothing at all*
    *is born,*
*dies, the shell says again*
    *and again*
*from the depth of hollowness.*
    *Its body*
*swept off by tide – so what?*
    *It sleeps*
*in sand, drying in sunlight,*
    *bathing*
*in moonlight. Nothing to do*
    *with sea*
*or anything else. Over*
    *and over*
*it vanishes with the wave.*

On one level a 'survivor' poem, inspiring in its moral grandeur, on another, surely important to the poet, expressing dramatically Zen's unfathomable emptiness. Here is the Chinese master Tao-hsin, Zen's Fourth Patriarch, in a sermon on 'Abandoning the Body':

The method of abandoning the body consists first in meditating on Emptiness ... Let the mind together with its world be quietened down to a perfect state of tranquillity; let thought be cast in the mystery of quietude, so that the mind is kept from wandering from one thing to another. When the mind is tranquillized in its deepest abode, its entanglements are cut asunder ... the mind in its absolute purity is the void itself. How almost unconcerned it appears ... Emptiness, non-striving, desirelessness, formlessness – this is true emancipation.

According to the great Taoist philosopher Chuang-tzu, his admirer, Tao-hsin said, 'Heaven and earth are one finger.' In the poem 'Hand' Takahashi writes, 'Snap my fingers – / time's no more.' He concludes, 'My hand's the universe, / it can do anything.' While such a poem may show indebtedness to masters like Tao-hsin, in a piece like the following, deceptively light, the poet's grasp is equally apparent:

AFTERNOON

*My hair's falling fast –*
*this afternoon*
*I'm off to Asia Minor.*

Always in Takahashi there is evidence of profound Zen, in itself distinguishing. His appeal, though, is by no means limited to Zennists, for his imagination has dizzying power: cosmic, surging through space and time ('Atom of thought, ten billion years – / one breath, past, present, future'), it pulls one beyond reality. At times, among his sparrows, he resembles the T'ang master Niao-k'e (Bird's Nest), so called because he meditated high in a tree, wise among the creatures.

Yet Takahashi is never out of this world, which for Zennists is a network of particulars, each reflecting the universal and taking reality from its relationship to all others: it has otherwise no existence. This doctrine of Interpenetration, as known in Zen and all other schools of Mahayana Buddhism, cannot be understood without being felt: to those incapable of feeling, such ideals have been thought mere 'mysticism'. Poets and philosophers have attempted for centuries to explain interdependence. Here is the late second-century Indian philosopher Pingalaka:

If the cloth had its own fixed, unchangeable self-essence, it could not be made from the thread ... the cloth comes from the thread and the thread from the flax . . . It is just like the . . . burning and the burned. They are brought together under certain conditions, and thus there takes place a phenomenon called burning . . . each has no reality of its own. For when one is absent the other is put out of existence. It is so with all things in this world, they are all empty, without self, without absolute existence. They are like the will-o'-the-wisp.

For one who believes in the interpenetration of all living things, the world is a body, and if he is a poet like Taka-hashi, troubled by what the unenlightened inflict upon one another, he will write:

> *Why this confusion,*
> *how restore the ravaged*
> *body of the world?*

And against this confusion he will invoke the saving force of Buddhism, the layman Vimalakirti who 'at a word draws galaxies to the foot of his bed', and Buddha himself, in a poem like 'Spinning Dharma Wheel', which ends:

> *Three thousand years since Buddha*
> *found the morning star – now*
> *sun itself is blinded by his light.*

The poet once wrote, 'We must model ourselves on Bodhidharma, who kept sitting till his buttocks grew rotten. We must have done with all words and letters, and attain truth itself.' This echo of Lao Tzu in the Taoist classic *Tao Teh Ching* ('He who knows does not speak') is, as truth, relative: to communicate his wisdom, Lao Tzu had to speak, and Takahashi's voice is inexhaustible. No one would question his seriousness, the near doctrinal tone of some of his work, yet his best poems pulse with *zenki* (Zen dynamism), flowing spontaneously from the formless self and partaking of the world's fullness:

CAMEL

*The camel's humps*
*shifted with clouds.*

*Such solitude beheads!*
*My arms stretch*

*beyond mountain peaks,*
*flame in the desert.*

V

Such are the three major phases of Zen poetry, spanning nearly 1,500 years from the earliest examples to the present, and displaying distinctive characteristics: the Chinese master Reito would very likely have appreciated Shinkichi Takahashi, much as Takahashi values Reito. This consistency, while very special, is by no means inexplicable. The philosophy underlying the poetry is today, in every respect, precisely what it was in T'ang China: it worked then, it works now, in the face of all that would seem bent on undermining it. In Japan, where industry is king, the need for Zen intensifies, and particular care is taken to preserve its temples and art treasures, numbered among the nation's glories.

Perhaps today Zen's spirit shines most purely in its poetry, some of which is familiar to all, wherever they happen to live and however limited their knowledge of the philosophy. Yet consciously or not, those who care for Fuyo-Dokai, Issa, Shinkichi Takahashi, *know* Zen – as much as those who revere Mu-ch'i and Sesshu. For to respond strongly to poetry and painting is to understand the source of their inspiration, just as to relate fully to others is to understand Zen's interpenetration – more completely than do those who, though familiar with its terminology, are incapable of attaining its spiritual riches. Walt Whitman, a poet much admired by Zennists, wrote in 'Song for Occupations':

> *We consider bibles and religions divine – I do not say*
> *     they are not divine,*
> *I say they have all grown out of you, and may grow out*
> *     of you still,*
> *It is not they who give the life, it is you who give the life,*
> *Leaves are not more shed from the trees, or trees from*
> *     the earth, than they are shed out of you.*

Zen always travelled well in time and space, through denying them. Its poetry will continue to move some to heroic efforts towards light, constantly delight others – which is as it should be. 'Zen is offering something,' the master Taigan Takayama said, 'and offering it directly. People just can't seem to grasp it.' Zen not only offers itself directly, but everywhere, and nowhere more authentically than in poems written in its name and honour, as the Chinese layman Sotoba realized 1,000 years ago when he wrote in his enlightenment:

> *The mountain – Buddha's body.*
> *The torrent – his preaching.*
> *Last night, eighty-four thousand poems.*
> *How, how make them understand?*

LUCIEN STRYK

In 1972, in my Introduction to the most recent of our co-translations of Zen poetry, I wrote: 'It is high time for Western intellectuals to turn more attention than ever to the appreciation of Zen poetry.' Since then the situation appears to have improved somewhat, as attested by a continuing demand for the collections of Zen poems in our rendering – above all, for Shinkichi Takahashi's poems. Heartened by our readers' favourable response, we set about preparing another co-translation two years ago, but my illness, critical at one time, prevented fruition of the project. Luckily enough, however, and thanks ultimately to Zen vitality in myself, this crisis has passed and we have finally succeeded in producing this book for the Western reader.

Our translation, I acknowledge, is often free, occasionally to such a degree that the reader, if he has a familiarity with the original language, may judge a good number of the pieces to be adaptations rather than translations. This may especially be felt with Takahashi. His original verse is sometimes pithy; at other times, lengthy and, one might almost say, prosaic. In the former case our rendering is verbally faithful to the originals; in the latter, some part is omitted, with the result that a number of the originals are turned into compact vignettes. This is the outcome of our policy on verse translation: translation is re-creation; and it is realized through Lucien Stryk's poetic intuition and linguistic skill. Our co-translation is finally Stryk's translation, as will be evident to the discerning eye of Western readers of poetry. Which leads me to say a few words on one aspect of the translation of Japanese/Chinese Zen poetry.

At present there can be few, if any, Japanese or Westerners capable of carrying out single-handedly this particular literary work. The requirements are clear: a would-be translator must possess rich practical experience of orthodox Zen, an ability to write English poetry, and a thorough knowledge of Japanese/Chinese literature. To satisfy just one of these requirements will demand many years, or indeed a lifetime, of training. That is why, as a second best, I have adopted the joint-translation method and, most fortunately, I have found in Lucien Stryk an unsurpassable collaborator. In the United States he is often described as a Zen poet, which appellation he fully deserves. It is not that he has subjected himself to regular discipline (Zen-sitting, etc.) in a Zen temple; rather, just as D. T. Suzuki once declared that his friend Kitaro Nishida, the noted Zen philosopher, had identified himself with Zen truth via sheer philosophical speculation, so Stryk has gained a high degree of Zen-identification by means of his poetical experience. Thus my own principal contribution to this joint translation is to supply Stryk with more or less literal translations and to examine his versions of the poems.

I have already touched upon Stryk's treatment of Takahashi's work: the concise, pithy rendering, whether of short or long pieces. His poetical genius is in its own way sufficiently flexible to adapt itself to any form of verse. Even so, he often seems to be particularly drawn to the shorter pieces and it is therefore appropriate that he has recently come to be attracted by *haiku*, and proposed to me that we devote a section of this book to them. In my opinion the *haiku* included here eminently satisfy a vital criterion of all good translations – that they possess a vigorous life of their own. The reader may find it interesting to compare the following versions, by nine different translators, of a *haiku* by Basho (N.B. numbers 3 and 6 are by Japanese translators; Stryk's is number 9):

1   *Ta'en ill while journeying, I dreamt*
    *I wandered o'er withered moor.*

2   *At midway of my journey fallen ill,*
        *To-night I fare again,*
    *In dream, across a desert plain.*

3   *Lying ill on journey*
    *Ah, my dreams*
    *Run about the ruin of fields.*

4   *Nearing my journey's end,*
    *In dreams I trudge the wild waste moor,*
    *And seek a kindly friend.*

5   *On a journey ta'en ill –*
    *My dream a dried-up plain,*
    *Through which I wander.*

6   *Taken ill on my travels,*
    *My dreams roam over withered moors.*

7   *On a journey, ill –*
        *and my dreams, on withered fields*
        *are wandering still.*

8   *Ailing on my travels,*
    *Yet my dream wandering*
    *Over withered moors.*

9   *Sick on a journey –*
    *over parched fields*
    *dreams wander on.*

There are several ways of reading Zen verse; for instance, the reader may approach it with *satori** as an object, or for critical appreciation, or simply for pleasure. In this respect, one probably should not be too rigorous; Zen verse should be accessible to all sorts of readers. But it appears to me that the days may not be very distant when English-speaking readers will find in Zen poetry a source of pure pleasure. I hope that this book will contribute to the creation of such an atmosphere.

In concluding this Note, my hearty thanks are due to the following:
Master Taigan Takayama of Yamaguchi and Master Bunpo Nakamura of Kyoto, learned young disciples of the late Abbot Zenkei Shibayama of Nanzenji Temple, Kyoto; the former furnished me with the Japanese-style readings of the Chinese Zennists' originals, frequently accompanying them with brief comments, whilst the latter enlightened me as to my questions about interpretation of some Chinese pieces, and obtained for us permission from the Daisen-in of Daitokuji Temple, Kyoto, to photograph Shinso's painting for this book.

The Zen poet Shinkichi Takahashi, who, though he happened to be taking a complete rest, clarified for me a term in one of his poems.

The friendly cooperation of the above Zennists has richly contributed towards securing for our book precision – not formal but essential – and attractiveness, both of which, I hope, will be counted among its features.

*In a suburb of Kyoto, Japan*     TAKASHI IKEMOTO
*November 1976*

* *Satori*: illumination or enlightenment; the state of consciousness of the Buddha-mind.

ACKNOWLEDGEMENTS

Thanks are due to the following for permission to reprint: *American Poetry Review*, *Bleb*, *Chariton Review*, *Chicago Review*, *Harbinger*, *Las Americas Review*, *Loon*, *Mr Cogito*, *Modern Poetry in Translation*, *The Mountain Path*, *New Letters*, *Northwest Review*, Patmos Press (from *the bell of transience*), *Prairie Schooner*, *Rapport*, Rook Press (from *Haiku of the Japanese Masters* and *The Duckweed Way*), Sceptre Press (from *Three Zen Poems*), Swallow Press (from *Selected Poems* by Lucien Stryk), *Thistle*.

If you study Japanese art, you see a man who is undoubtedly wise, philosophic and intelligent, who spends his time how? In studying the distance between the earth and the moon? No. In studying the policy of Bismarck? No. He studies a single blade of grass. But this blade of grass leads him to draw every plant and then the seasons, the wide aspects of the countryside, then animals, then the human figure. So he passes his life, and life is too short to do the whole.

*Vincent Van Gogh to his brother Theo – Arles, 1888*

*Part One*

# CHINESE POEMS OF ENLIGHTENMENT
# AND DEATH

NOTE: Most of the following Chinese masters and laymen, sixty in all, flourished during the Southern Sung dynasty (1127–1279), but their exact dates, with some exceptions, are missing in biographical records of Chinese Zennists. Among those who can be dated, Mumon-Ekai (Rinzai sectarian and author of *Mumonkan: The Gateless Barrier*, one of the most celebrated collections of disciplinary Zen questions and answers), Tendo-Nyojo (instructor in Soto Zen of Dogen, who, returning home from the continent, founded the Japanese Soto sect) and Daie-Soko (Rinzai Zen leader with a large following) stand out as brilliant figures in Chinese Zen history.

ENLIGHTENMENT


*Ox bridle tossed, vows taken,*
*I'm robed and shaven clean.*
*You ask why Bodhidharma came east –*
*Staff thrust out, I hum like mad.*

REITO


*Twenty years a pilgrim,*
*Footing east, west.*
*Back in Seiken,*
*I've not moved an inch.*

SEIKEN-CHIJU


*Once the goal's reached,*
*Have a good laugh.*
*Shaven, you're handsomer –*
*Those useless eyebrows!*

KISHU


*The old master held up fluff*
*And blew from his palm,*
*Revealing the Source itself.*
*Look where clouds hide the peak.*

KAIGEN

*The mountain – Buddha's body.*
*The torrent – his preaching.*
*Last night, eighty-four thousand poems.*
*How, how make them understand?*

LAYMAN SOTOBA (1036–1101)

*How long the tree's been barren.*
*At its tip long ropes of cloud.*
*Since I smashed the mud-bull's horns,*
*The stream's flowed backwards.*

HOGE

*Joshu's 'Oak in the courtyard' –*
*Nobody's grasped its roots.*
*Turned from sweet plum trees,*
*They pick sour pears on the hill.*

EIAN

*On the rocky slope, blossoming*
*Plums – from where?*
*Once he saw them, Reiun*
*Danced all the way to Sandai.*

HOIN

*Joshu's 'Oak in the courtyard'*
*Handed down, yet lost in leafy branch*
*They miss the root. Disciple Kaku shouts –*
*'Joshu never said a thing!'*

MONJU-SHINDO

*No dust speck anywhere.*
*What's old? new?*
*At home on my blue mountain,*
*I want for nothing.*

SHOFU

*Over the peak spreading clouds,*
*At its source the river's cold.*
*If you would see,*
*Climb the mountain top.*

HAKUYO

*Loving old priceless things,*
*I've scorned those seeking*
*Truth outside themselves:*
*Here, on the tip of the nose.*

LAYMAN MAKUSHO

*Traceless, no more need to hide.*
*Now the old mirror*
*Reflects everything – autumn light*
*Moistened by faint mist.*

SUIAN

*No mind, no Buddhas, no live beings,*
*Blue peaks ring Five Phoenix Tower.*
*In late spring light I throw this body*
*Off – fox leaps into the lion's den.*

CHIFU

*Sailing on Men River, I heard*
*A call: how deep, how ordinary.*
*Seeking what I'd lost,*
*I found a host of saints.*

SOAN

*In serving, serve,*
*In fighting, kill.*
*Tokusan, Ganto –*
*A million-mile bar!*

JINZU

*Years keeping* that *in mind,*
*Vainly questioning masters.*
*A herald cries, 'He's coming!'*
*Liver, gall burst wide.*

ANBUN

*Seamless –*
*Touched, it glitters.*
*Why spread* such *nets*
*For sparrows?*

GOJUSAN

*Clear, clear – clearest!*
*I ran barefoot east and west.*
*Now more lucid than the moon,*
*The eighty-four thousand*
*Dharma gates!*

MOAN

*I set down the emerald lamp,*
*Take it up – exhaustless.*
*Once lit,*
*A sister is a sister.*

GEKKUTSU-SEI

*Not falling, not ignoring –*
*A pair of mandarin ducks*
*Alighting, bobbing, anywhere.*

NAN-O-MYO

*How vast karma,*
*Yet what's there*
*To cling to? Last night,*
*Turning, I was blinded*
*By a ray of light.*

SEIGEN-YUIIN

*A deafening peal,*
*A thief escaped*
*My body. What*
*Have I learnt?*
*The Lord of Nothingness*
*Has a dark face.*

LAYMAN YAKUSAI

*A thunderbolt – eyes wide,*
*All living things bend low.*
*Mount Sumeru dances*
*All the way to Sandai.*

MUMON-EKAI (1183–1260)

*Where is the dragon's cave?*
*Dozing this morn in Lord Sunyata's*
*Palace, I heard the warbler.*
*Spring breeze shakes loose*
*The blossoms of the peach.*

KANZAN-SHIGYO

*No mind, no Buddha, no being.*
*Bones of the Void are scattered.*
*Why should the golden lion*
*Seek out the fox's lair?*

TEKKAN

*Earth, river, mountain:*
*Snowflakes melt in air.*
*How could I have doubted?*
*Where's north? south? east? west?*

DANGAI

*Joshu's word – Nothingness.*
*In spring blossom everywhere.*
*Now insight's mine,*
*Another dust-speck in the eye!*

KUCHU

*Joshu exclaimed, 'Dog's no Buddha,'*
*All things beg for life.*
*Even the half-dead snake*
*Stuffed in the basket.*
*Giving to haves, taking from*
*Have-nots – never enough.*

ICHIGEN

*Searching Him took*
*My strength.*
*One night I bent*
*My pointing finger –*
*Never such a moon!*

KEPPO

DEATH

*The fiery unicorn snapped*
*Its golden chain, moon-hare*
*Flung wide the silver gate:*
*Welcome, over Mount Shoȥan,*
*The midnight moon.*

DAICHU

*Seventy-six: done*
*With this life –*
*I've not sought heaven,*
*Don't fear hell.*
*I'll lay these bones*
*Beyond the Triple World,*
*Unenthralled, unperturbed.*

FUYO-DOKAI (1042–1117)

*A rootless tree,*
*Yellow leaves scattering*
*Beyond the blue –*
*Cloudless, stainless.*

SOZAN-KYONIN (9th century?)

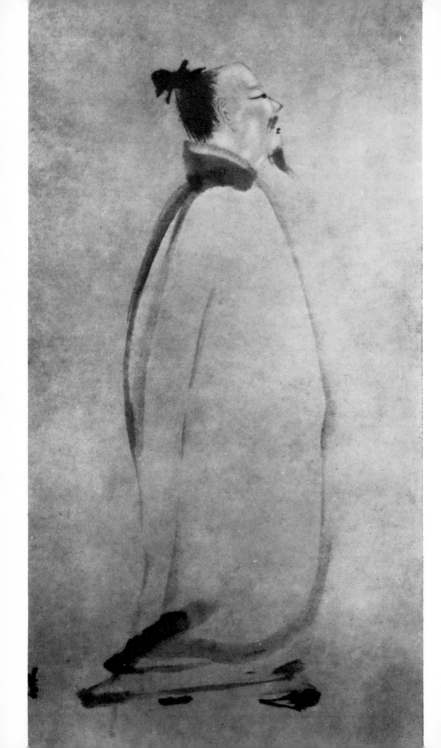

*Sixty-five years,*
*Fifty-seven a monk.*
*Disciples, why ask*
*Where I'm going,*
*Nostrils to earth?*

UNPO BUN-ETSU

*The word at last,*
*No more dependencies:*
*Cold moon in pond,*
*Smoke over the ferry.*

KOKO

*Sixty-six years*
*Piling sins,*
*I leap into hell –*
*Above life and death.*

TENDO-NYOJO (1163–1228)

*Sky's not high, earth not solid –*
*Try to see! Look,*
*This day, December 25th,*
*The Northern Dipper blazes south.*

SEIHO

*Way's not for the blind:*
*Groping, they might as well*
*Seek in the Dipper.*
*Old for Zen combat, only*
*The plough will comprehend:*
*I'll climb Mount Kongo, a pine.*

TOZAN-GYOSO

*'No mind, no Buddha,'*
*Disciples prattle.*
*'Got skin, got marrow.'*
*Well, goodbye to that.*
*Beyond, peak glows on peak!*

SHOZAN

*Nothing longed for,*
*Nothing cast off.*
*In the great Void —*
*A, B, C, D.*
*One blunder, another,*
*Everyone seeking*
*Western Paradise!*

LAYMAN YOKETSU

*Wino, always stumbling,*
*Yet in drinking*
*I show most discretion.*
*Where to wind up,*
*Sober, this evening?*
*Somewhere on the river bank*
*I'll find dawn's moon.*

HOMYO

*Sky-piercing sword, gleaming cold,*
*Cuts Demons, Buddhas, Patriarchs,*
*Then moonlit, stirred by wind, sinks*
*In its jewelled scabbard. Iron bulls*
*Along the river bank plunge everywhere.*

ZUIAN

*Talking: seven steps, eight falls.*
*Silent: tripping once, twice.*
*Zennists everywhere,*
*Sit, let the mind be.*

SHISHIN-GOSHIN (?–1339)

*High wind, cold moon,*
*Long stream through the sky.*
*Beyond the gate, no shadow –*
*Four sides, eight directions.*

SHOKAKU

*Today Rakan, riding an iron horse*
*Backwards, climbs Mount Sumeru.*
*Galloping through Void,*
*I'll leave no trace.*

RAKAN-KEINAN

*This fellow, perfect in men's eyes,*
*Utters the same thing over*
*And over, fifty-six years. Now*
*Something new – spear trees, sword hills!*

IKUO-JOUN

*No more head shaving,*
*Washing flesh.*
*Pile high the wood,*
*Set it aflame!*

CHITSU

*Forty-nine years –*
*What a din!*
*Eighty-seven springs –*
*What pleasures!*
*What's having? not having?*
*Dreaming, dreaming.*
*Plum trees snow-laden,*
*I'm ready!*

UNCHO

*Life's as we*
*Find it – death too.*
*A parting poem?*
*Why insist ?*

      DAIE-SOKO (1089–1163)

*Iron tree blooms,*
*Cock lays an egg.*
*Over seventy, I cut*
*The palanquin ropes.*

      WAKUAN-SHITAI (1108–69)

*Seventy-two years I've hung*
*The karma mirror.*
*Smashing through,*
*I'm on the Path!*

      IKUO-MYOTAN

All things come apart.
*No saintly sign*
*In these poor bones –*
*Strew their ashes*
*Onto Yangtze waves.*
*The First Principle, everywhere.*

      DAISEN

*Eighty-three years – at last*
*No longer muzzled.*
*The oak's a Buddha,*
*Void's pulled down.*

KYURIN-EKI

*Finally out of reach –*
*No bondage, no dependency.*
*How calm the ocean,*
*Towering the Void.*

TESSHO

*Fifty-three years*
*This clumsy ox has managed,*
*Now barefoot stalks*
*The Void – what nonsense!*

SEKISHITSU-SOEI

*Coming, I clench my hands,*
*Going, spread them wide.*
*Once through the barrier,*
*A lotus stem will*
*Drag an elephant!*

DANKYO-MYORIN (13th century)

*Seventy-eight awkward years –*
*A clownish lot. The mud-bull*
*Trots the ocean floor.*
*In June, snowflakes.*

ICHIGEN

*How Zennists carry on*
*About the birthless!*
*What madness makes me toll,*
*At noon, the midnight bell?*

GEKKO-SOJO

*This body won't pollute*
*The flowering slope –*
*Don't turn that earth.*
*What need a* samadhi *flame?*
*Heaped firewood's good enough.*

SEKIOKU-SEIKYO

*Mount Sumeru – my fist!*
*Ocean – my mouth!*
*Mountain crumbles, ocean dries.*
*Where does the jewelled hare leap,*
*Where reels the golden crow?*

KIKO

# Part Two

# POEMS OF THE JAPANESE
# ZEN MASTERS

*The Western Patriarch's doctrine is transplanted!*
*I fish by moonlight, till on cloudy days.*
*Clean, clean! Not a worldly mote falls with the snow*
*As, cross-legged in this mountain hut, I sit the evening through.*

DOGEN (1200–1253)

*Coming, going, the waterfowl*
*Leaves not a trace,*
*Nor does it need a guide.*

DOGEN

*The all-meaning circle:*
*No in, no out;*
*No light, no shade.*
*Here all saints are born.*

SHOICHI (1202–80)

*Clear in the blue, the moon!*
*Icy water to the horizon,*
*Defining high, low. Startled,*
*The dragon uncoils about the billows.*

RYUZAN (1274–1358)

*Invaluable is the Soto Way –*
*Why be discipline's slave?*
*Snapping the golden chain,*
*Step boldly towards the sunset!*

GASAN (1275–1365)

Many times the mountains have turned from green to yellow —
So much for the capricious earth!
Dust in your eyes, the triple world is narrow;
Nothing on the mind, your chair is wide enough.

MUSO (1275–1351)

Vainly I dug for a perfect sky,
Piling a barrier all around.
Then one black night, lifting a heavy
Tile, I crushed the skeletal void!

MUSO

At last I've broken Unmon's barrier!
There's exit everywhere — east, west; north, south.
In at morning, out at evening; neither host nor guest.
My every step stirs up a little breeze.

DAITO (1282–1337)

To slice through Buddhas, Patriarchs
I grip my polished sword.
One glance at my mastery,
The void bites its tusks!

DAITO

I moved across the Dharma-nature,
The earth was buoyant, marvellous.
That very night, whipping its iron horse,
The void galloped into Cloud Street.

GETSUDO (1285–1361)

*Thoughts arise endlessly,*
*There's a span to every life.*
*One hundred years, thirty-six thousand days:*
*The spring through, the butterfly dreams.*

DAICHI (1290–1366)

*Refreshing, the wind against the waterfall*
*As the moon hangs, a lantern, on the peak*
*And the bamboo window glows. In old age mountains*
*Are more beautiful than ever. My resolve:*
*That these bones be purified by rocks.*

JAKUSHITSU (1290–1367)

*He's part of all, yet all's transcended;*
*Solely for convenience he's known as master.*
*Who dares say he's found him?*
*In this rackety town I train disciples.*

CHIKUSEN (1292–1348)

*All night long I think of life's labyrinth –*
*Impossible to visit the tenants of Hades.*
*The authoritarian attempt to palm a horse off as deer*
*Was laughable. As was the thrust at*
*The charmed life of the dragon. Contemptible!*
*It's in the dark that eyes probe earth and heaven,*
*In dream that the tormented seek present, past.*
*Enough! The mountain moon fills the window.*
*The lonely fall through, the garden rang with cricket song.*

BETSUGEN (1294–1364)

*Beyond the snatch of time, my daily life.*
*I scorn the State, unhitch the universe.*
*Denying cause and effect, like the noon sky,*
*My up-down career: Buddhas nor Patriarchs can convey it.*

JUO (1296–1380)

*Magnificent! Magnificent!*
*No one knows the final word.*
*The ocean bed's aflame,*
*Out of the void leap wooden lambs.*

FUMON (1302–69)

*For all these years, my certain Zen:*
*Neither I nor the world exist.*
*The sutras neat within the box,*
*My cane hooked upon the wall,*
*I lie at peace in moonlight*
*Or, hearing water plashing on the rock,*
*Sit up: none can purchase pleasure such as this:*
*Spangled across the step-moss, a million coins!*

SHUTAKU (1308–88)

*Mind set free in the Dharma-realm,*
*I sit at the moon-filled window*
*Watching the mountains with my ears,*
*Hearing the stream with open eyes.*
*Each molecule preaches perfect law,*
*Each moment chants true sutra:*
*The most fleeting thought is timeless,*
*A single hair's enough to stir the sea.*

SHUTAKU

*Why bother with the world?*
*Let others go grey, bustling east, west.*
*In this mountain temple, lying half-in,*
*Half-out, I'm removed from joy and sorrow.*

RYUSHU (1308–88)

*After the spring song, 'Vast emptiness, no holiness',*
*Comes the song of snow-wind along the Yangtze River.*
*Late at night I too play the noteless flute of Shorin,*
*Piercing the mountains with its sound, the river.*

SHUNOKU (1311–88)

*How heal the phantom body of its phantom ill,*
*Which started in the womb?*
*Unless you pluck a medicine from the Bodhi-tree,*
*The sense of karma will destroy you.*

TESSHU (14th century)

*Not a mote in the light above,*
*Soul itself cannot offer such a view.*
*Though dawn's not come, the cock is calling:*
*The phoenix, flower in beak, welcomes spring.*

TSUGEN (1322–91)

*Men without rank, excrement spatulas,*
*Come together, perfuming earth and heaven.*
*How well they get along in temple calm*
*As, minds empty, they reach for light.*

GUCHU (1323–1409)

*Life: a cloud crossing the peak.*
*Death: the moon sailing.*
*Oh just once admit the truth*
*Of noumenon, phenomenon,*
*And you're a donkey-tying pole!*

MUMON (1323–90)

INSCRIPTION OVER HIS DOOR

*He who holds that nothingness*
*Is formless, flowers are visions,*
*Let him enter boldly!*

GIDO (1325–88)

*Riding backwards this wooden horse,*
*I'm about to gallop through the void.*
*Would you seek to trace me?*
*Ha! Try catching the tempest in a net.*

KUKOKU (1328–1407)

*The void has collapsed upon the earth,*
*Stars, burning, shoot across Iron Mountain.*
*Turning a somersault, I brush past.*

ZEKKAI (1336–1405)

*The myriad differences resolved by sitting, all doors opened.*
*In this still place I follow my nature, be what it may.*
*From the one hundred flowers I wander freely,*
*The soaring cliff – my hall of meditation*
*(With the moon emerged, my mind is motionless).*
*Sitting on this frosty seat, no further dream of fame.*
*The forest, the mountain follow their ancient ways,*
*And through the long spring day, not even the shadow of a bird.*

REIZAN (?–1411)

*Defying the power of speech, the Law Commission on Mount*
  *Vulture!*
*Kasyapa's smile told the beyond-telling.*
*What's there to reveal in that perfect all-suchness?*
*Look up! the moon-mind glows unsmirched.*

MYOYU (1333–93)

*My eyes eavesdrop on their lashes!*
*I'm finished with the ordinary!*
*What use has halter, bridle*
*To one who's shaken off contrivance?*

 EICHU (1340–1416)

*Last year in a lovely temple in Hirosawa,*
*This year among the rocks of Nikko,*
*All's the same to me:*
*Clapping hands, the peaks roar at the blue!*

HAKUGAI (1343–1414)

*Splitting the void in half,*
*Making smithereens of earth,*
*I watch inching towards*
*The river, the cloud-drawn moon.*

NANEI (1363–1438)

*Serving the Shogun in the capital,*
*Stained by worldly dust, I found no peace.*
*Now, straw hat pulled down, I follow the river:*
*How fresh the sight of gulls across the sand!*

KODO (1370–1433)

*For seventy-two years*
*I've kept the ox well under.*
*Today, the plum in bloom again,*
*I let him wander in the snow.*

BOKUO (1384–1455)

*After ten years in the red-light district,*
*How solitary a spell in the mountains.*
*I can see clouds a thousand miles away,*
*Hear ancient music in the pines.*

IKKYU (1394–1481)

VOID IN FORM

*When, just as they are,*
*White dewdrops gather*
*On scarlet maple leaves,*
*Regard the scarlet beads!*

IKKYU

FORM IN VOID

*The tree is stripped,*
*All colour, fragrance gone,*
*Yet already on the bough,*
*Uncaring spring !*

IKKYU

*Taking hold, one's astray in nothingness;*
*Letting go, the Origin's regained.*
*Since the music stopped, no shadow's touched*
*My door: again the village moon's above the river.*

KOKAI (1403–69)

*Only genuine awakening results in* that.
*Only fools seek sainthood for reward.*
*Lifting a hand, the stone lantern announces daybreak.*
*Smiling, the void nods its enormous head.*

NENSHO (1409–82)

*Unaware of illusion or enlightenment,*
*From this stone I watch the mountains, hear the stream.*
*A three-day rain has cleansed the earth,*
*A roar of thunder split the sky.*
*Ever serene are linked phenomena,*
*And though the mind's alert, it's but an ash heap.*
*Chilly, bleak as the dusk I move through,*
*I return, a basket brimmed with peaches on my arm.*

GENKO (?–1505)

ON JOSHU'S NOTHINGNESS

*Earth, mountains, rivers — hidden in this nothingness.*
*In this nothingness — earth, mountains, rivers revealed.*
*Spring flowers, winter snows:*
*There's no being nor non-being, nor denial itself.*

SAISHO (?–1506)

*Why, it's but the motion of eyes and brows!*
*And here I've been seeking it far and wide.*
*Awakened at last, I find the moon*
*Above the pines, the river surging high.*

YUISHUN (?–1544)

*Though night after night*
*The moon is stream-reflected,*
*Try to find where it has touched,*
*Point even to a shadow.*

TAKUAN (1573–1645)

*It's not nature that upholds utility.*
*Look! even the rootless tree is swelled*
*With bloom, not red nor white, but lovely all the same.*
*How many can boast so fine a springtide?*

GUDO (1579–1661)

*Whirled by the three passions, one's eyes go blind;*
*Closed to the world of things, they see again.*
*In this way I live; straw-hatted, staff in hand,*
*I move illimitably, through earth, through heaven.*

UNGO (1580–1659)

*Here none think of wealth or fame,*
*All talk of right and wrong is quelled:*
*In autumn I rake the leaf-banked stream,*
*In spring attend the nightingale.*

DAIGU (1584–1669)

*Who dares approach the lion's*
*Mountain cave? Cold, robust,*
*A Zen-man through and through,*
*I let the spring breeze enter at the gate.*

DAIGU

*Unfettered at last, a travelling monk,*
*I pass the old Zen barrier.*
*Mine is a traceless stream-and-cloud life.*
*Of those mountains, which shall be my home?*

MANAN (1591–1654)

*Only the Zen-man knows tranquillity:*
*The world-consuming flame can't reach this valley.*
*Under a breezy limb, the windows of*
*The flesh shut firm, I dream, wake, dream.*

FUGAI (17th century)

*The moon's the same old moon,*
*The flowers exactly as they were,*
*Yet I've become the thingness*
*Of all the things I see!*

BUNAN (1602–76)

*When you're both alive and dead,*
*Thoroughly dead to yourself,*
*How superb*
*The smallest pleasure!*

BUNAN

*Beware of gnawing the ideogram of nothingness:*
*Your teeth will crack. Swallow it whole, and you've a treasure*
*Beyond the hope of Buddha and the Mind. The east breeze*
*Fondles the horse's ears: how sweet the smell of plum.*

KARASUMARU-MITSUHIRO (1579–1638)

*Content with chipped bowl and tattered robe,*
*My life moves on serenely.*
*The single task: allaying hunger, thirst,*
*Indifferent to the murmurous world.*

TOSUI (?–1683)

*The seven seas sucked up together,*
*The dragon god's exposed.*
*Backwards flows the stream of Soto Zen:*
*Enlightened at last, I breathe!*

GESSHU (1618–96)

ON ENTERING HIS COFFIN

*Never giving thought to fame,*
*One troublesome span of life behind,*
*Cross-legged in the coffin,*
*I'm about to slough the flesh.*

BAIHO (1633–1707)

*One minute of sitting, one inch of Buddha.*
*Like lightning all thoughts come and pass.*
*Just once look into your mind-depths:*
*Nothing else has ever been.*

MANZAN (1635–1714)

*The town's aflame with summer heat,*
*But Mount Koma is steeped in snow.*
*Such is a Zen-man's daily life –*
*The lotus survives all earthly fire.*

TOKUO (1649–1709)

*Past, present, future: unattainable,*
*Yet clear as the moteless sky.*
*Late at night the stool's cold as iron,*
*But the moonlit window smells of plum.*

HAKUIN (1685–1768)

*Priceless is one's incantation,*
*Turning a red-hot iron ball to butter oil.*
*Heaven? Purgatory? Hell?*
*Snowflakes fallen on the hearth fire.*

HAKUIN

*How lacking in permanence the minds of the sentient –*
*They are the consummate nirvana of all Buddhas.*
*A wooden hen, egg in mouth, straddles the coffin.*
*An earthenware horse breaks like wind for satori-land.*

HAKUIN

*You no sooner attain the great void*
*Than body and mind are lost together.*
*Heaven and Hell – a straw.*
*The Buddha-realm, Pandemonium – shambles.*
*Listen: a nightingale strains her voice, serenading the snow.*
*Look: a tortoise wearing a sword climbs the lampstand.*
*Should you desire the great tranquillity,*
*Prepare to sweat white beads.*

HAKUIN

ON BASHO'S 'FROG'

*Under the cloudy cliff, near the temple door,*
*Between dusky spring plants on the pond,*
*A frog jumps in the water, plop!*
*Startled, the poet drops his brush.*

SENGAI (1750–1837)

*Without a jot of ambition left*
*I let my nature flow where it will.*
*There are ten days of rice in my bag*
*And, by the hearth, a bundle of firewood.*
*Who prattles of illusion or nirvana?*
*Forgetting the equal dusts of name and fortune,*
*Listening to the night rain on the roof of my hut,*
*I sit at ease, both legs stretched out.*

RYOKAN (1757–1831)

*My hands released at last, the cliff soars*
*Ten thousand metres, the ploughshare sparks,*
*All's consumed with my body. Born again,*
*The lanes run straight, the rice well in the ear.*

KANEMITSU-KOGUN (19th century)

*A blind horse trotting up an icy ledge –*
*Such is the poet. Once disburdened*
*Of those frog-in-the-well illusions,*
*The sutra-store's a lamp against the sun.*

KOSEN (1808–93)

*Madness, the way they gallop off to foreign shores!*
*Turning to the One Mind, I find my Buddhahood,*
*Above self and others, beyond coming and going.*
*This will remain when all else is gone.*

TANZAN (1819–92)

*It's as if our heads were on fire, the way*
*We apply ourselves to perfection of That.*
*The future but a twinkle, beat yourself,*
*Persist: the greatest effort's not enough.*

KANDO (1825–1904)

ON NEW YEAR'S DAY

*Fresh in their new wraps, earth and heaven,*
*And today I greet my eighty-first spring.*
*Ambition burning still, I grip my nandin staff.*
*Cutting through all, I spin the Wheel of Law.*

NANTEMBO (1839–1925)

*The question clear, the answer deep,*
*Each particle, each instant a reality,*
*A bird call shrills through mountain dawn:*
*Look where the old master sits, a rock, in Zen.*

SODO (1841–1920)

ON CLIMBING THE MOUNTAIN WHERE BUDDHA
TRAINED

*However difficult the cliff,*
*It's only after climbing one's aware.*
*Leisurely I followed Tathagata's footsteps.*
*Roaring below, a tiger chilled the day.*

MOKUSEN (1847–1920)

*Calm, activity – each has its use. At times*
*This worldly dust piles mountain-high.*
*Now the neighbour's asleep, I chant a sutra.*
*The incense burnt away, I sing before the moon.*

SOEN (1859–1919)

*Master Joshu and the dog –*
*Truly exorbitant, their foolishness.*
*Being and non-being at last*
*Annihilated, speak the final word!*

SOEN

ON VISITING SHORIN TEMPLE,
WHERE BODHIDHARMA ONCE LIVED

*The steep slope hangs above*
*The temple calm. An autumn voyager,*
*I go by ways neither old nor new,*
*Finding east, west the mind the same.*

SOEN

ON VISITING SOKEI, WHERE THE SIXTH PATRIARCH
LIVED

*The holy earth is overspread with leaves,*
*Wind crosses a thousand miles of autumn fields.*
*The moon that brushes Mount Sokei silvers,*
*This very instant, far Japan.*

TESSHU (1879–1939)

*Part Three*

# JAPANESE HAIKU

*To the willow –*
*all hatred, and desire*
*of your heart.*
                    BASHO (1644–94)

*Temple bell,*
*a cloud of cherry flowers –*
*Ueno? Asakusa?*

                              BASHO

*Cormorant fishing:*
*how stirring,*
*how saddening.*
                              BASHO

*Year's end –*
*still in straw hat*
*and sandals.*

                    BASHO

*Come, let's go*
*snow-viewing*
*till we're buried.*
                              BASHO

*Come, see*
*real flowers*
*of this painful world.*
                    BASHO

*Smell of autumn –*
*heart longs*
*for the four-mat room.*

BASHO

*Skylark*
*sings all day,*
*and day not long enough.*

BASHO

*Melon*
*in morning dew –*
*mud-fresh.*

BASHO

*June rain,*
*hollyhocks turning*
*where sun should be.*

BASHO

*Dozing on horseback,*
*smoke from tea-fires*
*drifts to the moon.*

BASHO

*Crow's*
*abandoned nest,*
*a plum tree.*

BASHO

Journey's end –
still alive,
this autumn evening.

BASHO

Wintry day,
on my horse
a frozen shadow.

BASHO

Shrieking plovers,
calling darkness
around Hoshizaki Cape.

BASHO

Withered grass,
under piling
heat waves.

BASHO

Autumn moon,
tide foams
to the very gate.

BASHO

Cedar umbrella,
off to Mount Yoshino
for the cherry blossoms.

BASHO

Autumn –
even the birds
and clouds look old.

BASHO

Year's end,
all corners
of this floating world, swept.

BASHO

Buddha's death-day –
old hands
clicking rosaries.

BASHO

To the capital –
snow-clouds forming,
half the sky to go.

BASHO

Old pond,
leap-splash –
a frog.

BASHO

Girl cat,
so thin
on barley and love.

BASHO

*Moor:*
*point my horse*
*where birds sing.*
BASHO

*Fish shop –*
*how cold the lips*
*of the salted bream.*
BASHO

*Autumn wind,*
*blasting the stones*
*of Mount Asama.*
BASHO

*Sick on a journey –*
*over parched fields*
*dreams wander on.*
BASHO

*Tomb, bend*
*to autumn wind –*
*my sobbing.*
BASHO

*Summer grasses,*
*all that remains*
*of soldiers' dreams.*
BASHO

*Full autumn moon –*
*on the straw mat,*
*pine shadow.*
        KIKAKU (1661–1707)

*Evening bridge,*
*a thousand hands*
*cool on the rail.*
        KIKAKU

*Sprinkle water wide –*
*for the sparrow,*
*the cicada.*
        KIKAKU

*Sacred night,*
*through masks*
*white breath of dancers.*
        KIKAKU

*Cicada chirp –*
*fan peddler*
*vaults a tree.*
        KIKAKU

*Above the boat,*
*bellies*
*of wild geese.*
        KIKAKU

May he who brings
flowers tonight,
have moonlight.

KIKAKU

Summer airing –
trying on a quilt,
strutting around.

KIKAKU

Leaf
of the yam –
raindrop's world.

KIKAKU

Shrine gate
through morning mist –
a sound of waves.

KIKAKU

A sudden chill –
in our room my dead wife's
comb, underfoot.

BUSON (1715–83)

Dew on the bramble,
thorns
sharp white.

BUSON

> *Through snow,*
> *lights of homes*
> *that slammed their gates on*
>     *me.*
>
> BUSON

*Ten holy nights –*
*even tea*
*chants* Namu Amida Butsu.

BUSON

> *My village –*
> *dragonflies,*
> *worn white walls.*
>
> BUSON

*In sudden flare*
*of the mosquito wick,*
*her flushed face.*

BUSON

> *Happy traveller:*
> *mosquito wick,*
> *moonlit grasses.*
>
> BUSON

*Wind in the west,*
*fallen leaves*
*gathering in the east.*

BUSON

*On the iris,*
*kite's*
*soft droppings.*

BUSON

*Short nap –*
*waking,*
*spring was gone.*

BUSON

*Miles of frost –*
*on the lake*
*the moon's my own.*

BUSON

*Over water,*
*sharp sickles*
*of reed gatherers.*

BUSON

*Mountains of Yoshino –*
*shedding petals,*
*swallowing clouds.*

BUSON

*Deer in rain –*
*three cries,*
*then heard no more.*

BUSON

*Swallows,*
*in eaves of mansions,*
*of hovels.*

BUSON

*Dewy morn –*
*these saucepans*
*are beautiful.*

BUSON

*Plum-viewing:*
*in the gay quarter*
*sashes are chosen.*

BUSON

*White lotus –*
*the monk*
*draws, back his blade.*

BUSON

*Plum scent*
*haloing*
*the moon.*

BUSON

*Such a moon —*
*the thief*
*pauses to sing.*

BUSON

*In the melon-patch*
*thief, fox,*
*meet head-on.*

TAIGI (1709–72)

*Beyond serenity,*
*grey kites*
*in twilight.*

TAIGI

*Barley's season —*
*dust mutes*
*the midday bell.*

TAIGI

*Temple in*
*deep winter grove,*
*a bonfire's glow.*

TAIGI

*Zazen:*
*fat mosquitoes*
*everywhere.*

TAIGI

*In the boat,*
*crescent moon's light*
*in my lap.*

TAIGI

*Fallen leaves –*
*raking,*
*yet not raking.*

TAIGI

*Thunder –*
*voices of drowned*
*in sunken ships.*

TAIGI

*Swellfish eaten,*
*he chants* nembutsu
*in his sleep.*

TAIGI

*Cherry blossoms?*
*In these parts*
*grass also blooms.*

ISSA (1763–1827)

*Over paddies*
*at its foot,*
*smoke of Mount Asama.*

ISSA

*Changing clothes,*
*but not*
*the wanderer's lice.*
　　　　ISSA

*Owls are calling,*
*'Come, come,'*
*to the fireflies.*
　　　　ISSA

*Tonight you too*
*are rushed,*
*autumn moon.*
　　　　ISSA

*Just by being,*
*I'm here –*
*in snow-fall.*
　　　　ISSA

*Autumn wind,*
*the beggar looks*
*me over, sizing up.*
　　　　ISSA

*Lost in bamboo,*
*but when moon lights –*
*my house.*
　　　　ISSA

*Buddha Law,*
*shining*
*in leaf dew.*
     ISSA

          *A good world,*
          *dew-drops fall*
          *by ones, by twos.*
             ISSA

*Listen,*
*all creeping things –*
*the bell of transience.*
     ISSA

          *Don't weep, insects –*
          *lovers, stars themselves,*
          *must part.*
             ISSA

*Cuckoo sings*
*to me, to the mountain,*
*in turn.*
     ISSA

          *Flies swarming –*
          *what do they want of*
          *these wrinkled hands?*
            'ISSA

*Where there are humans
you'll find flies,
and Buddhas.*

ISSA

*One bath
after another –
how stupid.*

ISSA

*Farmer,
pointing the way
with a radish.*

ISSA

*Winter lull –
no talents,
thus no sins.*

ISSA

*Short night –
scarlet flower
at vine's tip.*

ISSA

*Let's take
the duckweed way
to clouds.*

ISSA

*Buddha's Nirvana,*
*beyond flowers,*
*and money.*

ISSA

*First cicada:*
*life is*
*cruel, cruel, cruel.*

ISSA

*Autumn evening –*
*knees in arms,*
*like a saint.*

ISSA

*At prayer,*
*bead-swinging*
*at mosquitoes.*

ISSA

*When plum*
*blooms –*
*a freeze in hell.*

ISSA

*Don't fly off, nightingale –*
*though your song's poor,*
*you're mine.*

ISSA

*Five yen each:*
*a cup of tea,*
*the nightingale.*

ISSA

*What a world,*
*where lotus flowers*
*are ploughed into a field.*

ISSA

*Fireflies*
*entering my house,*
*don't despise it.*

ISSA

*I'm leaving —*
*now you can make love,*
*my flies.*

ISSA

*Nightingale's song*
*this morning,*
*soaked with rain.*

ISSA

*Kites shriek*
*together —*
*departure of the gods.*

ISSA

*Children,*
*don't harm the flea,*
*with children.*

ISSA

*Borrowing my house*
*from insects,*
*I slept.*

ISSA

*Clouds of mosquitoes –*
*it would be bare*
*without them.*

ISSA

*About the field*
*crow moves*
*as if he's tilling.*

ISSA

*Autumn wind –*
*mountain's shadow*
*wavers.*

ISSA

*Watch it – you'll bump*
*your heads*
*on that stone, fireflies.*

ISSA

*My hut,*
*thatched*
*with morning glories.*

ISSA

*Skylarks singing –*
*the farmer*
*makes a pillow of his hoe.*

ISSA

*Never forget:*
*we walk on hell,*
*gazing at flowers.*

ISSA

*Outliving*
*them all, all –*
*how cold.*

ISSA

*In this world*
*even butterflies*
*must earn their keep.*

ISSA

*As we grow old,*
*what triumph*
*burning mosquitoes.*

ISSA

*Cuckoo's crying –*
*nothing special to do,*
*nor has the burweed.*

ISSA

*From the bough*
*floating down river,*
*insect song.*

ISSA

*Closer, closer*
*to paradise –*
*how cold.*

ISSA

*Worldly sky –*
*from now on*
*every year's a bonus.*

ISSA

*First firefly,*
*why turn away –*
*it's Issa.*

ISSA

*Under cherry trees*
*there are*
*no strangers.*

ISSA

*Be respectful,*
*sparrows,*
*of our old bedding.*

ISSA

*Dew spread,*
*the seeds of hell*
*are sown.*

ISSA

*Mokuboji Temple –*
*fireflies come even*
*to the barking dog.*

ISSA

*In my house*
*mice and fireflies*
*get along.*

ISSA

*Cries of wild geese,*
*rumours*
*spread about me.*

ISSA

*Shush, cicada –*
*old Whiskers*
*is about..*

ISSA

Geese, fresh greens
wait for you
in that field.

ISSA

Treated shabbily
by fleas, by flies,
day quits.

ISSA

From burweed,
such a butterfly
was born?

ISSA

When I go,
guard my tomb well,
grasshopper.

ISSA

Reflected
in the dragonfly's eye –
mountains.

ISSA

A poor quarter:
flies, fleas, mosquitoes
live forever.

ISSA

*No need to cling*
*to things —*
*floating frog.*
      JOSO (1662–1704)

                    *About the grave*
                    *waves of spring mist —*
                    *I barely live.*

                              JOSO

*These branches*
*were the first to bud —*
*falling blossoms.*

      JOSO

                    *Gruel heaped*
                    *in a perfect bowl —*
                    *sunlight of New Year's Day.*
                              JOSO

*How green —*
*flowering slopes*
*reflect each other.*

      JOSO

                    *Writing,*
                    *rubbing it out —*
                    *face of poppy.*
                         HOKUSHI (1665–1718)

My house gutted –
well, the cherry flowers
had fallen.

        HOKUSHI

Sailboats in line,
island
lost in mist.

        HOKUSHI

Woman –
how hot the skin
she covers.

    LADY SUTE-JO (1633–98)

Are there
short-cuts in the sky,
summer moon?

        LADY SUTE-JO

Contending –
temple bell,
winter wind.

      KITO (1740–89)

Nightingale,
rarely seen,
came twice today.

        KITO

*Barley-reaping song,*
*smith's hammer,*
*mingling.*

KITO

*Seaweed*
*between rocks —*
*forgotten tides.*

KITO

*How cool,*
*forehead touched*
*to green straw-mat.*

LADY SONO-JO (1649–1723)

*Shameful*
*these clothes —*
*not one stitch mine.*

LADY SONO-JO

*After dream,*
*how real*
*the iris.*

SHUSHIKI (1669–1725)

*Frost of separation —*
*father, child*
*under one quilt.*

SHUSHIKI

Even in my town
now, I sleep
like a traveller.
  KYORAI (1651–1704)

After the green storm,
true colour
of the rice-paddy.
  KYORAI

Melon –
how well
it keeps itself.
  RANSETSU (1654–1707)

Each morn
from the straw raincoat
put out to dry – fireflies.
  RANSETSU

Travelling
old armour,
a glistening slug.
  RANSETSU

Five rice dumplings
in bamboo leaves –
no message, no name.
  RANSETSU

*Fly, dare take*
*the rice grain*
*on my chin.*

RANSETSU

*Autumn wind –*
*across the fields,*
*faces.*

ONITSURA (1660–1738)

*Plum blossoms –*
*one's nose,*
*one's heart.*

ONITSURA

*Summer airing –*
*on one pole,*
*a shroud.*

KYOROKU (1655–1715)

*Even the dumplings*
*are smaller –*
*autumn wind.*

KYOROKU

*Night snow,*
*neighbour's cock*
*sounds miles away.*

SHIKO (1665–1731)

*Arid fields,*
*the only life –*
*necks of cranes.*

SHIKO

*Small fish-boats,*
*after what*
*as snow covers my hat?*

SHIKO

*First snow –*
*head clear,*
*I wash my face.*

ETSUJIN (1656–1739)

*Nightingale –*
*my clogs*
*stick in the mud.*

BONCHO (?–1714)

*Piled for burning,*
*brushwood*
*starts to bud.*

BONCHO

*Late spring:*
*paling rose,*
*bitter rhubarb.*

SODO (1641–1716)

*Sudden shower,*
*cooling lava*
*of Mount Asama.*
SODO

*Morning frost,*
*Mount Fuji*
*brushed lightly.*
TANTAN (1674–1761)

*On the rock*
*waves can't reach,*
*fresh snow.*
TANTAN

*Quivering together –*
*ears of barley,*
*butterfly.*
LADY KANA-JO (17th century)

*One sneeze –*
*skylark's*
*out of sight.*
YAYU (1701–83)

*Transplanting rice,*
*he pisses*
*in a crony's field.*
YAYU

*Whales*
*bellowing dawn,*
*in icy waters.*
GYODAI (1732–93)

*Inching*
*from dark to dark –*
*seaslug.*
GYODAI

*Slowly*
*over cedars,*
*sunshine, showers.*
GYODAI

*Forty years –*
*how sharp*
*the insect's cry.*
SHIRAO (1735–92)

*Mountain mist –*
*torches dropped*
*as clouds redden.*
SHIRAO

*Moonlit night –*
*by melon flowers,*
*fox sneezes.*
SHIRAO

*Were it not for*
*cries in snow,*
*would the herons be?*
LADY CHIYO-JO (1701–75)

*In the well-bucket,*
*a morning glory –.*
*I borrow water.*
LADY CHIYO-JO

*Pure brush-clover –*
*basket of flowers,*
*basket of dew.*
RYOTA (1707–87)

*On rainy leaves*
*glow*
*of the village lights.*
RYOTA

*Tea-kettle,*
*hooked mid-air*
*towards heaven.*
HAKUIN (1685–1768)

*Cherry blossoms –*
*so many,*
*I'm bent over.*
SOBAKU (1728–92)

Mirrored by stream,
swallow darts —
a fish.
    SAIMARO (1656–1737)

> Green, green, green —
> herbs splash
> the snow-field.
>     RAIZAN (1654–1716)

Cloud above lotus —
it too
becomes a Buddha.
    BORYU (18th century)

> Night frost —
> pulsing wings
> of mandarin ducks.
>     SOGI (1421–1502)

Cherry blossoms
dizzying —
my painful neck.
    SOIN (1604–82)

> Cold, yes,
> but don't test
> the fire, snow Buddha.
>     SOKAN (1458–1546)

*Nameless,*
*weed quickening*
*by the stream.*
    CHIUN (15th century)

        *Buddha:*
        *cherry flowers*
        *in moonlight.*
           HOITSU (1760–1828)

*Moving*
*deep into mist,*
*chrysanthemums.*
    SAMPU (1647–1732)

        *Morning glory,*
        *so pure*
        *the dew's unseen.*
           KAKEI (1648–1716)

*Chirping –*
*grasshopper*
*in the scarecrow's sleeve.*
LADY CHIGETSU (17th century)

        *Spring plain,*
        *gulped*
        *by the pheasant's throat.*
           YAMEI (18th century)

*Long summer rains –*
*barley's tasteless*
*as the sky.*
  MOKUSETSU (17th century)

> *Cry of the deer –*
> *where at its depths*
> *are antlers?*
>     OTSUYU (1674–1739)

*Skylark*
*soaring – her young*
*will starve.*
      SORA (1649–1710)

> *Wild geese –*
> *fellow travellers,*
> *all the way to Ise.*
>   LADY CHINE-JO (17th century)

*Returning*
*by an unused path –*
*violets.*
      BAKUSUI (1720–83)ʼ

> *My old thighs –*
> *how thin*
> *by firelight.*
>     SHISEKI (1676–1759)

*Shameful —*
*dead grass*
*in the insect's cage.*
            SHOHA (?–1771)

                    *Guest gone,*
                    *I stroke the brazier,*
                    *talk to myself.*
                            SHOZAN (1717–1800)

*When bird passes on —*
*like moon,*
*a friend to water.*
        MASAHIDE (1657–1723)

                    *Barn's burnt down —*
                    *now*
                    *I can see the moon.*
                            MASAHIDE

*Imagine —*
*the monk took off*
*before the moon shone.*
        SHIKI (1867–1902)

                    *Thing long forgotten —*
                    *pot where a flower blooms,*
                    *this spring day.*
                            SHIKI

*Storm – chestnuts*
*race along*
*the bamboo porch.*

SHIKI

*Dew, clinging*
*to potato field,*
*the Milky Way.*

SHIKI

*Stone*
*on summer plain –*
*world's seat.*

SHIKI

*Autumn wind:*
*gods, Buddha –*
*lies, lies, lies.*

SHIKI

*Wicker chair*
*in pinetree's shade,*
*forsaken.*

SHIKI

*Aged nightingale –*
*how sweet*
*the cuckoo's cry.*

SHIKI

*Summer sky*
*clear after rain –*
*ants on parade.*

SHIKI

*Heath grass –*
*sandals*
*still fragrant.*

SHIKI

*Among Saga's*
*tall weeds,*
*tombs of fair women.*

SHIKI

*Evening bell:*
*persimmons pelt*
*the temple garden.*

SHIKI

*Autumn come –*
*cicada husk,*
*crackling.*

SHIKI

*Indian summer:*
*dragonfly shadows seldom*
*brush the window.*

SHIKI

Midnight sound –
leap up:
a fallen moonflower.

SHIKI

Sudden rain –
rows of horses,
twitching rumps.

SHIKI

White butterfly
darting among pinks –
whose spirit?

SHIKI

Such silence:
snow tracing wings
of mandarin ducks.

SHIKI

# Part Four

# SHINKICHI TAKAHASHI (b. 1901), CONTEMPORARY JAPANESE MASTER

SHELL

*Nothing, nothing at all*
    *is born,*
*dies, the shell says again*
    *and again*
*from the depth of hollowness.*
    *Its body*
*swept off by tide – so what?*
    *It sleeps*
*in sand, drying in sunlight,*
    *bathing*
*in moonlight. Nothing to do*
    *with sea*
*or anything else. Over*
    *and over*
*it vanishes with the wave.*

MUSHROOM

*I blow tobacco smoke*
*into her frozen ear.*
*A swallow darts above.*

*Pleasures are like mushrooms,*
*rootless, flowerless,*
*shoot up anywhere.*

*A metal ring hangs*
*from her ear, mildew*
*glowing in the dark.*

## FLIGHT OF THE SPARROW

*Sparrow dives from roof to ground,*
*a long journey – a rocket soars*
*to the moon, umpteen globes collapse.*

*Slow motion: twenty feet down, ten billion*
*years. Light-headed, sparrow does not think,*
*philosophize, yet all's beneath his wings.*

*What's Zen? 'Thought,' say masters,*
*'makes a fool.' How free the brainless*
*sparrow. Chirrup – before the first 'chi',*

*a billion years. He winks, another. Head left,*
*mankind's done. Right, man's born again.*
*So easy, there's no end to time.*

*One gulp, swallow the universe. Flutter*
*on limb or roof – war, peace, care banished.*
*Nothing remains – not a speck.*

*'Time's laid out in the eavestrough,'*
*sparrow sings,*

> *pecks now and then.*

## SKY

*Climbing the wax tree*
*to the thundering sky,*
*I stick my tongue out –*
*what a downpour!*

SPARROW IN WITHERED FIELD

*Feet pulled in, sparrow dead*
*under a pall of snow.*
*' Sparrow's a red-black bird,'*
*someone says, then –*
*' sun's a white-winged bird.'*

*If the bird sleeps, so will man:*
*things melt in air, there's only breathing.*
*You're visible, nose to feet,*
*and while an ant guard rams a 2-by-4*
*genitals saunter down the road.*

*Budge them, they'll roll over –*
*pour oil on them, light up.*

*Atom of thought, ten billion years –*
*one breath, past, present, future.*

*Wood's so quiet. I cover my ears –*
*how slowly the universe crumbles.*

*Snow in withered field, nothing to touch.*
*Sparrow's head clear as sky.*

AFTERNOON

*My hair's falling fast –*
*this afternoon*
*I'm off to Asia Minor.*

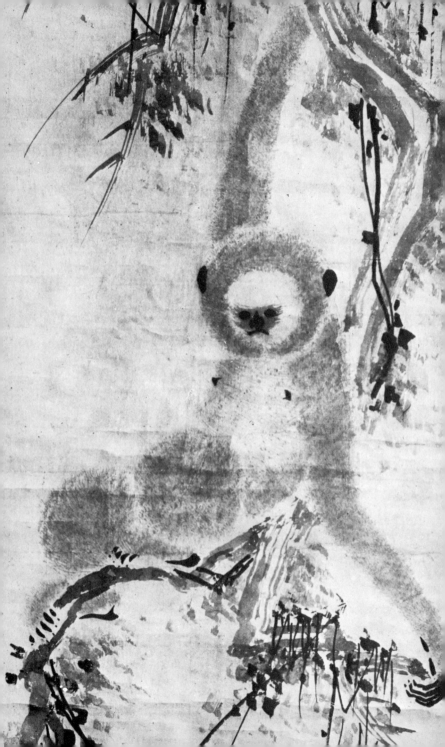

HAND

*I stretch my hand –*
*everything disappears.*

*I saw in the snake-head*
*my dead mother's face,*

*in ragged clouds*
*grief of my dead father.*

*Snap my fingers –*
*time's no more.*

*My hand's the universe,*
*it can do anything.*

SWEET POTATO

*Of all things living*
*I'd be a sweet potato,*
*fresh dug up.*

CAMEL

*The camel's humps*
*shifted with clouds.*

*Such solitude beheads!*
*My arms stretch*

*beyond mountain peaks,*
*flame in the desert.*

## RAW FISH AND VEGETABLES

*When unborn, my mother minced*
*time with her rusty knife –*
*rain-soft, grained like cod-roe.*
*When ready, I burst from her womb.*

*Nothing better to do, I try*
*to relive that first house:*
*no one else there, however I*
*kicked touching nothing in*
*darkness – mite in a whale.*

*Posterity aeons hence, listen:*
*time's a white radish, pickled,*
*yellowing. My father swam that*
*vinegar's raw fish and vegetables.*

## DOWNY HAIR

*Charmed by a girl's soft ears,*
*I piled up leaves and burnt them.*

*How innocent her face*
*in rising smoke – I longed*

*to roam the spiral of those ears,*
*but she clung stiffly*

*to the tramcar strap, downy*
*hair fragrant with leafsmoke.*

TOAD

*' The instant he boarded the plane*
*Toad was in London' –* wrong.

*Toad's unaware of distance,*
*between his belly and man's,*
*between himself, the crushing wheel.*

*' Shrinking utterly, he's nowhere' –* right.

*London, Tokyo flattened by webbed feet*
*all at once. In the marsh – no distance, sound –*
*a scaly back is overgrown with moonflowers.*

DRIZZLE

*Cat runs the dripping fence,*
*melts into green shade*
*hollow as thought lost.*

*Earth in a claw of dead cat,*
*guts strewn on pavement –*
*time, those needle eyes.*

*In the garret three kittens lap.*
*An old woman, like a crumpled bill,*
*tries to recall cat's name.*

SEA OF OBLIVION

*Future, past, the sea*
*of oblivion,*
*with present capsized.*

*Sun splits the sea*
*in two –*
*one half's already bottled.*

*Legs spread on the beach,*
*a woman feels*
*the crab of memory*

*crawl up her thigh.*
*Somewhere*
*her lover drowns.*

*Sand-smeared, bathing*
*in dreams,*
*the young leap against each other.*

CLOUD

*I'm cheerful, whatever happens,*
*a puff in sky –*
*what splendour exists, I'm there.*

MOTHER AND I

*While boats list in port*
*sunset ripens*
*the forest of Hakone.*

*Men fall like raindrops.*
*I perch on*
*a chair, open my umbrella.*

*Cloud-burst. Smiling, mother*
*sits up in*
*her coffin. Ages ago.*

*Tomorrow Columbus will reach*
*(was it?)*
*Venezuela, this hand*

*will embrace or kill – takes*
*but a finger.*
*Under white sail, the universe.*

## SHEEP

*Awaking on grass, sheep, goat*
*stay put – how fine doing nothing.*
*Crow points from dead branch.*

*Sheep could care less – life, death,*
*all one where she lies*
*soft warm wool. Goat bleats,*

*horns sun-tipped. What's better*
*than warmth? sheep muses, sharing*
*her wonder with goat, with crow.*

## ETERNITY

*Ice on eaves, sparrow melts in my head,*
*cracked shapeless, no hint of brain.*

*Sparrow's long journey. Now road flowers,*
*young girls breasting wheat.*

*(Once fry shot upstream towards clouds.)*

*Sparrow blinked: drifting on the moonlit sea,*
*a woman, legs octopus arms, waves biting*

*to black eyes. No need to grasp, no rim,*
*depth, shallowness – sun's steering*

*round the navel, galaxies whirl the spine.*
*Snow's hip-high, thighs stiff with frost.*
*(Sweet as fish, how fresh death's breeze.)*

SPARROW AND BIRD-NET BUILDING

*Sparrow's always sleeping –*
*meanwhile*
*a building surrounds him.*

*Snoop, shoot up the*
*elevator,*
*quite alone: the building's*

*a pinch of dust. No day,*
*night,*
*so light strikes from*

*his throat, under a wing*
*glow*
*sun, moon, stars. No one's here,*

*no one's expected for a billion*
*years.*
*Sparrow dreams, sparrow knows.*

CLAY IMAGE

*Near the shrine, humped back,*
*bird on pole – eyes, warm*
*as folded wings, reflect*
*the penumbra of the universe.*

*On the horizon,*
*a cylindrical building,*
*once bird, now mud and stone.*

*Birth's a crack in the*
*ground plan. Since universe*
*is no bigger than its head,*
*where's the bird to fly?*

*Who says bird's eyelashes*
*are short? A lump,*
*time rolled from nostril.*

*Cooling the bird's hot tongue,*
*the unglazed red clay image.*

*Its eyes dark, and in their*
*cavities –*
*minute vibrations, earthquakes.*

GODS

*Gods are everywhere:*
*war between Koshi and Izumo*
*tribes still rages.*

*The all of All, the One*
*ends distinctions.*

*The three thousand worlds*
*are in that plum blossom.*
*The smell is God.*

BRAGGART DUCK

*Duck lives forever,*
*daily. Waking, he finds*
*he's slept a billion years.*

*The very centre of the*
*universe, he has no use*
*for eyes, ears, feet.*

*What need for one*
*who knows his world*
*of satellite stations?*

*Freed from time,*
*changeless. Duck's not*
*sharp as dog shooting*

*through space, a rocket.*
*Besides he's*
*been there already.*

STONE WALL

*Flower bursts from stone,*
*in rain and wind*
*dog sniffs and aims a leak.*
*Butterfly-trace through haze*
*where child splashes.*

*Over the paper screen,*
*a woman's legs, white, fast.*
*No more desire, I'm content.*

*Later I saw her, hands*
*behind her back —*
*repulsing nothing really,*
*welcoming sun*
*between her thighs.*

*Near the stone wall,*
*a golden branch.*

BEACH

*Gale: tiles, roofs whirling,*
*disappearing at once.*

*Rocks rumble, mountains*
*swallow villages,*
*yet insects, birds chirp by*
*the shattered bridge.*

*Men shoot through space,*
*race sound. On TV nations*
*maul each other, endlessly.*

*Why this confusion,*
*how restore the ravaged*
*body of the world?*

MOON AND HARE

*Things exist alone.*
*Up on the moon*
*I spot Hare*

*in a crater*
*pounding rice to cakes.*
*I ask for one.*

*'What shape?' says Hare.*
*'One like a rocket.'*
*'Here – take off!'*

*Up and out,*
*pass everything*
*at once,*

*free at last –*
*unaware of*
*where I'm heading.*

## LAP DOG

*Lap dog in a cloth-wrapped box,*
*moist eyes, nose,*
*I tote you in place*
*of your evaporated mistress.*

*I'd like to brew down, devour,*
*ten thousand mini-skirted legs.*

*Body torn, yet spirit's whole,*
*no knife can reach it.*
*Dawn breaks from her buttocks.*

*Runaway tramcar thunders by,*
*sun-flash! Fling*
*the lap dog down a manhole.*

*Ha! Sun-blade's in her back.*

## MOON

*Moon shines while billions*
*of corpses rot*
*beneath earth's crust.*
*I who rise from them,*
*soon to join them – all.*
*Where does moon float?*
*On the waves of my brain.*

VIMALAKIRTI

*Vimalakirti, Vaishali*
*millionaire, sutra hero,*
*in bed in his small space –*

*while you're sick,*
*I'll lie here.*
*Revive, I'm whole.*

*Illness, a notion,*
*for him body is sod, water –*
*moves, a fire, a wind.*

*Vimalakirti, layman hero,*
*at a word draws galaxies*
*to the foot of his bed.*

SNOWY SKY

*The blackbird swooped,*
*eyes shadowing earth, dead leaves,*
*feathers tipped with snow.*

*One finds beaches anywhere,*
*airports, skies of snow.*

*Perched on the ticket counter,*
*blackbird watches*
*the four-engined plane land,*
*propellers stilled.*

*Dead leaves flutter from the sky.*

NEAR SHINOBAZU POND

*A bream swam by the tramcar window,*
*the five-tiered pagoda bright in rain.*

*On the telephone wire, sparrow —*
*amused, in secret dialogue.*

*Voiceless, rock glimmers with*
*a hundred million years.*

*Day before yesterday, the dead sparrow*
*hopped on the fish-tank*

*where froth-eyed salamander*
*and a tropic fish curled fins.*

*The sparrow, spot of rose among*
*the lotus leaves, stirs evening air.*

LET'S LIVE CHEERFULLY

*Dead man steps over sweaty sleepers*
*on the platform, in quest of peace.*

*Thunderously dawn lights earth.*

*Smashed by the train, head spattered*
*on the track – not a smudge of brain.*

*Nothing left: thought – smoke.*
*A moment – a billion years.*

*Don't curl like orange peel, don't ape*
*a mummified past. Uncage eternity.*

*When self's let go, universe is all –*
*O for speed to get past time!*

ROCKS

*Because the stake was driven*
*in that rice paddy,*
*world was buried in mud.*

*Rocks dropped like birds*
*from the crater:*
*being is mildew spread on non-being.*

*Rocks that were women stand,*
*wooden stakes, everywhere,*
*give birth to stones.*

*No-minds – whirling, flying off, birds.*

URN

*Autumn blast – wild boar*
*limps, one leg dead grass.*
*Bird sings, feathers tattered,*
*eyes stiff twigs.*
*Boar gives his own.*

*As those bronze cavities*
*decay, he fuses into rock,*
*sets it and bird to flame,*
*and meteors to the sky.*

*Boar flashes on the sun,*
*red tail severed, scorching:*
*urn, inlaid with gold*
*and silver, holds the image.*

*Through night, glittering*
*with millet seeds,*
*boar shoots, a comet.*

SPRING

*Spring one hundred years ago*
*was very warm: it's in my*
*palm, such life, such gaiety.*

*Future is a bird streaking*
*aimlessly, past is dregs –*
*everything's here, now.*

*Thought sparking thought*
*sparking thought: headlands*
*pocked by time, the ram of tides.*

*Rock rising, rock sinking.*
*No space, what was is nowhere –*
*a hundred years hence,*

*spring will be as warm.*

## PEACH BLOSSOM AND PIGEON
(painting by Kiso)

*Pink petals of peach blossom,*
*blue/green pigeon's head,*

*eyes bamboo slits, rainbow*
*wings fold in all history.*

*Black tail down, you fly to*
*future's end, beyond the sun.*

*To clear the air, make sweetest*
*scent, you bulge your breast.*

*Branch in your coffee-coloured claws,*
*wait till phantom bubbles burst around.*

## SPINNING DHARMA WHEEL

*A stone relief I never tire of:*
*life-sized Buddha, broken nose,*
*hair spiralling, eyes serene moons,*
*chipped mudra-fingers at the breast,*
*legs crossed in lotus. Under each arm*
*a red line streams – warm blood.*
*Around the halo, angels among flowers,*
*on either side, beasts, open-mouthed,*
*on guard. He turns the treasure wheel.*
*Three thousand years since Buddha*
*found the morning star – now*
*sun itself is blinded by his light.*

FOUR DIVINE ANIMALS

*Snake swam across the blue stream.*
*You've seen its slough – your own?*

*Tiger in the white bamboo, eyes hard:*
*learn from this – to see death*
*is to see another, never oneself.*

*Flames char the bamboo grove,*
*the vermilion sparrow has flown*
*into a fossil – just like that.*

*Tortoise moves, a slow fire,*
*down hill, flushed in sunset –*
*claws death to shreds, red, brown.*

*Tiger's soft tongue laps a dragon*
*from the sea. Sparrow, riding*
*a shell-tank, makes for its belly.*

*What's this? My body's shaking with laughter.*

A LITTLE SUNLIGHT

*Trees in the wood lifeless,*
*leaves pall the earth.*
*On a large drift the red-sweatered*

*woman waits. There's just*
*a blink of sun, a leaf blows*
*on her face. The man comes up*

*quietly, lies down beside her.*
*Soon she takes off alone,*
*toting her case. He prays*

*(I hear him now) all may go well*
*with her. A plane roars above,*
*he snuffs his cigarette.*

*Two dead leaves blow apart.*

EXPLOSION

*I'm an unthinking dog,*
*a good-for-nothing cat,*
*a fog over gutter,*
*a blossom-swiping rain.*

*I close my eyes, breathe –*
*radioactive air! A billion years*
*and I'll be shrunk to half,*
*pollution strikes my marrow.*

*So what – I'll whoop at what*
*remains. Yet scant blood left,*
*reduced to emptiness by nuclear*
*fission, I'm running very fast.*

RAILROAD STATION

*A railroad station, a few*
*passengers getting on, off,*
*a closed stall on the platform.*

*Is it there or in my head,*
*floating on the creases*
*of my brain? No need to stay*

*or leave, a place so quiet:*
*ticket window, wicket, employees –*
*none. But there's a samurai*

*committing suicide. Station*
*master cocks the camera's eye,*
*proof of his diligence.*

*Train skims rails of my brain,*
*what's hanging to that strap*
*is briefcase, camera, no man.*

ABSENCE

*Just say, ' He's out' –*
*back in*
*five billion years!*